Rough and Smooth

by Emily C. Dawson

amicus readers

Say hello to amicus readers.

You'll find our helpful dog, Amicus, chasing a ball—to let you know the reading level of a book.

(A)

 1

 2

Learn to Read
Frequent repetition of sentence structures, high frequency words, and familiar topics provide ample support for brand new readers. Approximately 100 words.

Read Independently
Repetition is mixed with varied sentence structures and 6 to 8 content words per book are introduced with photo label and picture glossary supports. Approximately 150 words.

Read to Know More
These books feature a higher text load with additional nonfiction features such as more photos, time lines, and text divided into sections. Approximately 250 words.

Amicus Readers are published by **Amicus**
P.O. Box 1329, Mankato, Minnesota 56002

U.S. publication copyright © 2012 Amicus.
International copyright reserved in all countries.
No part of this book may be reproduced in any
form without written permission from the publisher.

Printed in the United States of America at Corporate
Graphics, in North Mankato, Minnesota.

Series Editor   Rebecca Glaser
Series Designer   Christine Vanderbeek
Photo Researcher   Heather Dreisbach

Library of Congress Cataloging-in-Publication Data
Dawson, Emily C.
Rough and smooth / by Emily C. Dawson.
pages cm. — (Amicus Readers. Let's compare)
Includes index.
Summary: "Compares and contrasts common rough and
smooth objects, both in nature and man-made. Includes
comprehension activity"–Provided by publisher.
ISBN 978-1-60753-002-2 (library binding)
1. Surface roughness—Juvenile literature.
2. Materials—Texture—Juvenile literature. I. Title.
TA418.7.R87 2012
620.1'1292–dc22
                                                    2010041754

Photo Credits
Kutt Niinepuu/Dreamstime.com, Cover-top, 12t, 20b; Mark Evans/iStockphoto, Cover-bottom, 12b, 21b; Benjamin Christie, 4; Vladimir Ovchinnikov, 6t; Christian Musat, 6b; Bradcalkins/Dreamstime.com, 8t, 20m; John James Henderson/Dreamstime.com, 8b; Alanpoulson/Dreamstime.com, 10t; Medicimage Medicimage/Photolibrary, 10b; TommL/iStockphoto, 14t, 21m; Eric Michaud/iStockphoto, 14b, 20t; John Murray, 16t, 21t; Gjs/Dreamstime.com, 16b; Ross Anania/GettyImages, 18; Arcady31/Dreamstime.com, 22tl; woraput chawalitphon/iStockphoto, 22ml; Severija/Dreamstime.com, 22bl; Michael Kempf, 22tr; Nataliia Tsukanova/Dreamstime.com, 22mr; absolut_100/iStockphoto, 22br

1025   3-2011
10 9 8 7 6 5 4 3 2 1

Let's Compare!

Table of Contents

* Sweet Potato, cumin + Sa
* Calzone filled w bacon, Av
dried Tomatos + Brie
* Cheesy Polenta cake topp
eggplant, sundried tomatos
* Chicken, prosciutto, capsicu
* Ricotta + Parmesan Tai
roasted cherry tomatos + Sa
* Freerange poached egg w
aioli on pastry
* House made baked Bean
and corn Bread
* Salmon, caper + spring o
* Roasted capsicum, eggplant
* Scrambled eggs wrapped in
pastry w herb mayonaise
* Mushroom, caramelized On
* Salad =

Let's compare rough and smooth.

Rough things are bumpy.

Smooth things are flat.

rough

Let's Compare!

smooth

6

An elephant has rough skin. A dolphin has smooth skin. Its skin feels like rubber.

rough

Let's Compare!

smooth

8

An oak tree is rough. Its bark splits. A birch tree has smooth bark. Its bark stretches.

rough

Let's Compare!

smooth

10

A pineapple is rough.

Mom cuts off the skin.

An apple is smooth.

Cody eats the whole

apple.

rough

Let's Compare!

smooth

12

A monster truck
has rough tires.
A racecar has smooth
tires. Smooth tires help
racecars go fast.

rough

Let's Compare!

smooth

Jen's running shoes have rough soles. Amy's ballet shoes have smooth soles. Amy dances on the smooth floor.

rough

Let's Compare!

smooth

Steve rubs wood with rough sandpaper. Joe writes on smooth notebook paper.

Let's Compare!

18

Rough things have bumps. Smooth things are flat. What do you see that is rough or smooth?

Picture Glossary

ballet →
a dance performed
to music with set
movements

← **bark**
the tough outer covering
of a tree

monster truck →
a giant pickup truck with
huge wheels

← sandpaper
paper covered with grains of sand used to make wood or other surfaces smooth

sole →
the bottom of a shoe

← tire
the rubber part of a wheel that is filled with air

21

Rough and Smooth

Look at the photos.
1. Which things are rough?
2. Which things are smooth?
3. Which things go together?

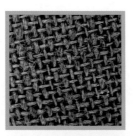

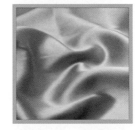

amicus
readers

Ideas for Parents and Teachers

Let's Compare, an Amicus Readers Level A series, lets children compare opposites. Repetitive sentence structures, high frequency words, and photo labels provide appropriate support for new readers. In each book, the picture glossary defines new vocabulary and the "Let's Compare" activity page reinforces compare and contrast techniques.

Before Reading
- Ask the child about the difference between rough and smooth.
- Discuss the cover photos. What do these photos tell them?
- Look at the picture glossary together. Ask the child to sort the photos into a rough group and a smooth group.

Read the Book
- "Walk" through the book and look at the photos. Let the child ask questions about the photos.
- Read the book to the child, or have him or her read independently.
- Show the child how to refer to the picture glossary and read the photo labels to understand the full meaning.

After Reading
- Have the child identify rough and smooth elements in each photograph.
- Prompt the child to think more, asking questions such as What other things can you think of that are rough? What other things are smooth? Can you think of any other words to describe rough or smooth?

23

Index

Web Sites

How Stuff Works: Fun Physics Activities for Kids
http://home.howstuffworks.com/fun-physics-activities-for-kids.htm/printable

Neuroscience for Kids: Touch Experiments
http://faculty.washington.edu/chudler/chtouch.html